My Name is
_____

On the day of the coronation,

— date: ————————

I will be :
_____

Hello children,
I have some exciting news to share with you! On September 8th, 2022, Prince Charles, the son of Queen Elizabeth II, became the King of the United Kingdom of Great Britain and Northern Ireland.

The Coronation of His Majesty King Charles III's coronation will take place on Saturday 6 May 2023 at Westminster Abbey in London. Where this tradition has been held for over 900 years. It is sure to be a grand and memorable event!

Keep your eyes open for news and updates on this historic moment in British history.

During the ceremony, he will wear the Crown of St. Edward on his head. This crown was moved from the Tower of London in December and adjusted to fit the size and shape of the new king's head. According to Buckingham Palace, this will be the same crown that was used in the coronation of King Henry III in the year 1220.

God save King Charles III

Can you believe how old and special this crown is? I can't wait to see King Charles III wearing the Crown of St. Edward during his coronation ceremony on May 6th at Westminster Abbey. It will be a truly historic moment!

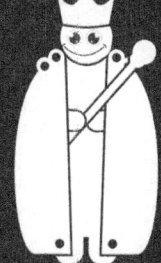

King Charles III, the new king of the United Kingdom! He was born on November 14th, 1948, and is the oldest of Queen Elizabeth's four children.

At the age of 73, he became the oldest British monarch to ascend the throne. That's quite an impressive accomplishment.

LONDON

I hope you're excited to learn more about King Charles III and his reign as the new king. Stay tuned for more updates and news!

Printed in Great Britain
by Amazon